Contents

Contents

Welcome

1

Welcome

Welcome to **PhotoPlus X7** from **Serif**—more than ever, the best value in image creation and editing software for any enthusiast and those new to digital photography, whether at home, in school, an organization or growing business. PhotoPlus is the number one choice for working with photographs and paint-type images, whether for the web, multimedia, printing, or archiving as keepsakes.

PhotoPlus has the features you'll need... from importing or creating pictures, through manipulating colours, making image adjustments, applying filter effects and so much more, all the way to final export. Built-in support for most modern digital cameras makes it easy to open your very own digital photos, either as JPG or as unprocessed raw images.

PhotoPlus also offers powerful on-computer post-shoot development, using **Import Raw**, where you're in full control of your raw image's white balance and exposure, and perform "blown" highlight recovery. For image corrections, adjustments, filter effects (including stunning artistic effects), or layer cutouts, try **Lens Correction**, **PhotoFix**, **Filter Gallery**, and **Cutout Studio**, respectively. There is also an impressive range of standalone adjustments and advanced editing tools to help you get the very best from your images.

PhotoPlus and PhotoPlus Organizer: a powerful combination

PhotoPlus takes care of all your image creation and photo editing needs. However, if you're looking to take a step back from photo editing and manage your collection of photos, scanned images, etc. you can use PhotoPlus Organizer. This is installed automatically with PhotoPlus, and offers a powerful platform for launching your photos in PhotoPlus.

You'll be able to sort, group, rate, and tag your photos, filter your photos for display by several methods, and share them online.

Registration

Don't forget to register your new copy, using the **Registration Wizard** on the **Help** menu. That way, we can keep you informed of new developments and future upgrades!

New features

Professional adjustments and controls

- **Lab colour mode for professional edits made easy** (see p. 105)
  Lab colour mode is a major advance that processes images in a high-quality, natural colour space. Lightness and contrast adjustments can be made without dramatically changing colours, and hues can be adjusted and accentuated without affecting contrast, so you can make striking enhancements with a real world feel.

- **Lens Correction studio** (see p. 44)
  A new filter that combines lens distortion, lens vignette and chromatic aberration corrections for improved results. Also straighten images and correct perspective in this 'studio' before moving back to the main workspace to carry out contrast, colour, or other fixes and creative enhancements.

- **Improved Clarity adjustment now also smooths** (see p. 47)
  The Clarity adjustment can now also use its contrast-awareness to smooth areas of similar colour while maintaining sharp lines and areas of high detail.

Creative effects

- **New Blend Modes for special effects** (see p. 31)
  Vivid Light, Hard Mix and Pin Light blend modes join the
  range of other professional ways of combining the colour and
  brightness of layered images.

- **Warp Studio** (see p. 62)
  Improved warp brushes are faster and more accurate in the new
  dedicated Warp Studio, which also features better Undo, masks
  to protect areas of the image, and warp meshes that you can
  save and apply to other photos.

- **New Halftone Screen effect** (see p. 51)
  Give photos a fresh look with a brand new Halftone Screen
  effect that includes line screen and circular screen options, ideal
  for giving your photos a very retro look!

- **Stylish new effects presets** (see p. 46)
  PhotoFix now includes a new Photography category featuring
  vintage presets, adjusting colour, contrast, and quality.

Easier to use, plus other improvements

- **Startup Assistant for easy access and learning** (see p. 11)
  The new-look starting point for your photo editing provides a
  wealth of **cross-product news** and PhotoPlus-specific video
  tutorials, written tutorials, help, and Tips & Tricks that updates
  at regular intervals. The assistant keeps track of unread articles
  so you won't miss a thing! An Open option also gives you
  access to all your existing work, based on document history.

- **Restore last session**
  If you prefer to skip the Startup Assistant and its new learning
  resources, you can restore your last session with PhotoPlus
  opening with the same file(s) as last time you used it.

- **Improved quality**
  Some important technologies in PhotoPlus have been improved to give you a higher quality display while you're editing, and higher quality brushes that support larger sizes and smoother drawing. These changes make PhotoPlus even more useful for increasingly-large digital photos!

- **Broad support for scanners and digital cameras** (see p. 18)
  As manufacturers have been very slow to introduce 64-bit versions of their scanner drivers, PhotoPlus has been updated to support both 32-bit and any newer 64-bit drivers (whether you're running either the 32-bit or 64-bit version of PhotoPlus). WIA-compliant imaging devices are also supported, and the Raw Studio now also opens files from an even bigger range of high end digital cameras.

- **New look for tabs**
  The user interface tabs have been given a makeover with a modern, flat look. They now also respond better to being resized, with sliders and other adjustments fitting to the available space.

- **Save as JPG XR**
  JPG XR has become a recognised standard format and is supported by PhotoPlus when opening, saving, and exporting images. This file type supersedes Microsoft HD Photo WDP and HDP files, which are still supported.

- **New Clone Tool pick-up preview** (see p. 91)
  After cloning the source area, the Clone Tool shows the "picked up" pixels directly under the clone brush before applying. Great for a visual indication of how the cloned region will look on the target area.

Installation

Installing PhotoPlus follows different procedures depending on whether you are installing from disc or via download.

You can install your new version alongside previous versions and use them independently.

32 or 64-bit PhotoPlus X7 installs to respective 32 or 64-bit computers.

Installation procedure (from disc)

- Insert your purchased disc into your disc drive.

  - If AutoPlay is enabled on the drive, this automatically starts the Setup Wizard. Follow the on-screen instructions for install.

    -or-

  - If AutoPlay is not enabled (or doesn't start the install automatically), navigate to your program disc and double-click **autorun.exe**.

Installation procedure (from download)

- From serif.com, when logged into your Serif account, follow the on-screen instructions to download.

System requirements

Minimum:

- Windows-based PC* with DVD drive and mouse

- Operating system:
  Microsoft Windows® XP SP3 (32 bit)
  Windows® Vista (32 or 64 bit)
  Windows® 7 (32 or 64 bit)
  Windows® 8 (32 or 64 bit)

- 512MB RAM (1GB RAM for 64-bit operation)

- 448MB free hard disk space (including PhotoPlus Organizer).

- 1024 x 768 monitor resolution (DPI 100%)

* Main processor must support SSE2 instructions

Recommended:

- Additional disk resources and memory are required when editing large and/or complex images

- To fully enjoy the enhancements in X7, a multi-core processor, 64-bit edition of Windows 8/7/Vista, and 3GB or more RAM are recommended

Optional:

- Windows-compatible printer

- Scanner and/or digital camera (TWAIN/WIA compatible)

- Pen (graphics) tablet

- Internet account and connection required for product updates and accessing online resources

Opening, Saving and Organizing

2

Startup Assistant

Once PhotoPlus has been installed, you're ready to start.

- For Windows Vista/7: Setup adds a **Serif PhotoPlus X7** item to the **All Programs** submenu of the Windows **Start** menu. Use the Windows **Start** button to pop up the Start menu, click on **All Programs** and then click **Serif PhotoPlus X7**.

- For Windows 8: The Setup routine during install adds a **Serif PhotoPlus X7** entry to the desktop and also to the Start screen. Double-click the PhotoPlus icon from the desktop, or click the PhotoPlus tile on the Start screen.

On program launch, the Startup Assistant is displayed which offers different routes into PhotoPlus.

The options are described as follows:

The default home page keeps you in touch with Serif promotions and showcases articles (tutorials, etc.) You can also view the PhotoPlus Overview and Quick Start video.

To access images and PhotoPlus files, as well as creating HDR photo merges and scanned images.

Creates a new image from scratch.

Opens **PhotoPlus Organizer** to manage and filter photos for PhotoPlus.

For online video/written tutorials, help, tips & tricks, and more—all via an updating feed that can be filtered. The Product Help and your electronic PhotoPlus X7 User Guide are also provided.

For cross-product news, company news, and product announcements, using Serif's news feed.

Any time you access the Startup Assistant, the Learn or News buttons indicate the number of new articles to be viewed (if available). This number will decrease as you read each article in the Learn or News pane. When new articles arrive, these will be indicated the next time you open the Startup Assistant.

Any new unread article arriving in the Learn or News pane will display a "new" indicator in its thumbnail.

 Once you've clicked on a new article the "new" indicator changes to a "read" indicator.

Don't forget to use the keyword Search box at the top-right of the Startup Assistant.

This is an incredibly powerful tool for filtering specific file names, Learn articles, or News articles.

To access the Startup Assistant when PhotoPlus is already running, choose **Startup Assistant** from the **File** menu.

Starting from scratch

PhotoPlus lets you create an image from scratch which is based on a pre-defined canvas size (e.g., 10 x 8 in). Different canvas size options are available from a range of categories (International/US Paper, Photo, Video, Web, or Animation). You can also create your own custom canvas sizes, and even store them for future use. For either preset or custom sizes, the resolution can be set independently of canvas size.

When you create a new image, you can choose to work in different colour modes, i.e., RGB, Lab, or Greyscale, in either 8- or 16-bits/channel. Use a **Bit Depth** of 16 bit for higher levels of image detail.

To create a new image (via Startup Assistant):

1. Open PhotoPlus to display the Startup Assistant.
    - or -

    Select **Startup Assistant** from the **File** menu (during your session).

2.   Select **New Image**.

3.   In the New Image dialog, you can either:

    i.   For a **preset** canvas size, select a suitable **Category** from the drop-down list. Categories are named according to how your image or animation is intended to be used, e.g. pick a Photo category for photo-sized canvases.

    ii.   Pick a canvas **Size** from the drop-down list.
      - or -

    •   For a custom canvas size, enter your own **Width** and **Height**. If the dimensions are non-standard, the Size drop-down list will be shown as "Custom." For future use, save the custom size with **Add Size** (from the ▼ button) if necessary.

> Although you can resize the image **canvas size** (width x height) later, it's usually best to allow some extra canvas area at first.

4.   (Optional) Add a **Resolution** for the new image file. Leave the resolution as it is unless you're sure a different value is required.

5.   (Optional) Select a **Colour Mode**, choosing to operate in RGB, Lab, or Greyscale mode.

6.   (Optional) Select a **Bit Depth** of 16 bits per channel for projects which require higher levels of colour detail. Otherwise a bit depth of 8 bits/channel is used as default.

7.   (Optional) Select a background type in the **Background** drop-down list.

    •   When painting from scratch, you'll normally choose White.

    •   You can also choose Background Colour, to use the current background colour shown on the Colour tab.

- When creating an animation, Transparent is often ideal.

8. When you've made your selections, click **OK.**

To create a new picture or animation (during your session):

1. Click [icon] **New** on the **Standard** toolbar.

2. In the New Image dialog, set your canvas size (see p. 70) and then check **Animation** to create an animation or leave unchecked for a picture.

3. Click **OK**. The new image or animation opens in a separate untitled window.

Opening an existing file

You can use the Startup Assistant's **Open** button to access files recently viewed in PhotoPlus or any file on your computer. PhotoPlus opens all the standard formats for print and web graphics, in addition to its native SPP format, Adobe Photoshop (PSD) files, and Paint Shop Pro (PSP) files.

Raw files open in an Import Raw dialog, which offers image adjustment on the "undeveloped" image before opening. See Adjusting raw images in PhotoPlus Help. Similarly, you can create HDR merged images from the Startup Assisant (Open>Create) and even readjust your HDR merge results from a saved intermediate HDR image.

Once you've created and saved your project as a PhotoPlus file, it can also be opened from the Startup Assistant.

Opening an image

1. Open PhotoPlus to display the initial Startup Assistant.

    - or -

    Select **Startup Assistant** from the **File** menu (during your session).

2. Select **Open**.

3. Select **All Images** from the Browse My Computer pane.

4. From the dialog, locate and select your file, then click **Open**.

Opening saved PhotoPlus work

1. Open PhotoPlus to display the initial Startup Assistant.

2. Select **Open**.

3.   Several options are possible:

   i.   For recently opened PhotoPlus files (and images), select a thumbnail from the main pane.

   ii.   The photo opens in your workspace.

- or -

   •   For any other previously saved work, select **PhotoPlus Files** from the Browse My Computer pane.

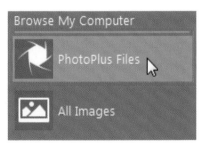

   iii.   From the dialog, locate and select your file, then click **Open**.

To open any photo (without Startup Assistant):

   •   Click **Open** on the **Standard** toolbar.

Getting images from TWAIN/WIA devices

If your digital camera or scanner supports either the TWAIN or WIA standard, you can bring pictures from these devices directly into PhotoPlus.

For 64-bit PhotoPlus, you'll be able to use native 64-bit or 32-bit sources, without leaving the program.

For TWAIN/WIA device-specific setup, see device documentation.

To acquire your image (from Startup Assistant):

1. Open PhotoPlus to display the initial Startup Assistant.
   - or -

   Select **Startup Assistant** from the **File** menu (during your session).

2. Select **Open**.

3. Select **Import from TWAIN** from the Browse My Computer pane.

4. (For multiple devices) Select the device from the dialog, and press **OK**.

5. Complete the procedure using the displayed acquisition dialog associated with the selected source.

You can also import scanned images directly via **File>Import>Acquire**.

To select a TWAIN or WIA source for scanning (during your session):

1. From the **File** menu's **Import** flyout. click either **Select TWAIN Source** or **Select WIA Source**.

2. From the dialog, which differs for TWAIN and WIA devices, select a device and click **OK**.

Saving a file

PhotoPlus lets you work on (and save) one of several file types:

- A **PhotoPlus Picture** (**SPP**) file is project-based and so preserves 'project' information (e.g., layers, masks, paths), if present, when saving the file.

- For a currently open **image** file you can edit and save the image back to its original format.

- An intermediate **HDR** image can be saved, which stores the results of an HDR Photo Merge for future use.

To save your PhotoPlus Picture (SPP):

- Click the 💾 **Save** button on the **Standard** toolbar, or to save under a different path or base name, choose **File>Save As**.

To save your currently open image:

- If you've altered the background layer only and no layers, paths, or masks have been added, you can save (without prompt) the altered image to its current base name via **Save** and **Save As**.
  - or -

- If you've added layers, paths, etc, when you click a **Save** option you'll be asked if you want to keep the project information.

  - In the dialog, click **Yes** to save your project information (as an SPP file).
    - or -
    Click **No** to save as a flattened image (i.e., without layers).

To revert an image file:

- Click **Revert** from the **File** menu.

Using plug-ins

PhotoPlus supports **non-automated** Adobe Photoshop-compatible plug-in filters (e.g., Topaz and Filter Forge plug-ins), which, if located in your PhotoPlus Plugins folder, will appear on the **Effects** menu.

 32-bit plug-ins will only run in 32-bit PhotoPlus and 64-bit plug-ins in 64-bit PhotoPlus.

To apply a plug-in filter:

- Choose it from **Effects>Plugin Filters**. Either the effect will be applied immediately, or the plug-in will display its own dialog.

Organizing photos

PhotoPlus Organizer is Serif's powerful photo management application which acts as an essential launch point for your photos into PhotoPlus.

To launch Organizer:

1. Open PhotoPlus to display the Startup Assistant.

2. Select **Organizer**. Organizer is launched as a separate application.
   - or –

- From the **Standard** toolbar, select 🌐 **Organizer**.

PhotoPlus Organizer is a great starting point for editing photos in PhotoPlus. Click 🖼 **Edit in PhotoPlus** on Organizer's toolbar to open, then edit, your chosen photo.

Layers, Masks and Blending

3

Introduction to layers

If you're accustomed to thinking of pictures as flat illustrations in books, or as photographic prints, the concept of **image layers** may take some getting used to. However, they are one of the most powerful features in PhotoPlus, allowing you to adjust and manipulate your photos in a variety of ways in a non-destructive environment.

Think of layers as transparent sheets upon which you can add adjustments, effects filters, paint colours, and add further images, shapes, and text to build up the perfect picture.

Kinds of layers

In a typical PhotoPlus image—for example, a photograph you've scanned in, a new picture file you've just created, or a standard bitmap file you've opened—there is one layer that behaves like a conventional "flat" image. This is called the **Background layer**, and you can think of it as paint overlaid on an opaque, solid colour surface.

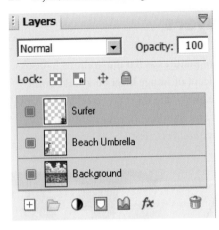

Using the **Layers** tab, you can create any number of new layers in your image. Each new one appears on top of the currently active layer, comprising a stack that you can view and manipulate with the Layers tab. We call these additional layers **standard layers** to differentiate them from the Background layer. Standard layers behave like transparent sheets through which the underlying layers are visible.

Other types of layers also exist in PhotoPlus:

- **Shape layers** are specifically designed to keep drawn lines and shapes (including QuickShapes) separate from the other layers so that they remain editable. (See Drawing and editing lines and shapes; p. 92)

- **Text layers** work like Shape layers, but are intended exclusively for text. (See Creating and editing text; p. 98)

- **Fill layers** contain an adjustable solid colour or gradient fill.

- **Adjustment layers** apply corrective image adjustments to lower layers. (See Using adjustment layers; p. 38)

- **Filter layers**, are much like standard layers, but you can apply one or more filter effects to the layer without permanently altering layer content. You also have full control over effects in the future. (See Using filter layers; p. 51)

Selections and layers

With few exceptions, you will work on just one layer at any given time—click a layer on the Layers tab to activate and work on that layer. Tools and commands generally affect the entire active layer. However, if there's a selection in place, tools and commands are limited to the pixels inside the selection.

Selections are independent from layers. They don't actually include image content—they just describe a region with boundaries. Therefore, if your image has multiple layers and you switch to another layer, the selection stays in place and follows you to the new active layer.

Operations involving layers

To carry out basic layer operations:

- To select a layer, click on its name in the Layers tab. The selected layer is now the **active layer**. Note that each layer's entry includes a preview thumbnail, which is visible at all times and is especially useful when identifying layer contents.

- ⊞ To create a new standard layer above the active layer, click the **New Layer** button on the Layers tab. Dragging a file from Windows Explorer and dropping it onto the current window also creates a new layer from the dragged image.

- Click the ◑ **New Fill or Adjustment Layer** button to apply a **Fill Layer** or an image adjustment layer.

- The ▢ **Add Layer Mask** button adds a mask to the currently selected layer (not a Background layer).

- The **Add Layer Depth Map** button creates a depth map for the selected layer (not a Background layer).

- The **Add Layer Effects** button creates a 2D or 3D effect on the layer (not a Background layer). Right-click to copy/paste, clear or hide effects.

- To make a layer's contents visible or invisible, click the **Hide/Show Layer** button next to its name on the Layers tab.

- To convert any shape, text or fill layer to a standard layer, right-click on the layer name and choose **Rasterize** from the menu.

- To convert the Background layer to a standard layer (which supports transparency), right-click "Background" on the Layers tab and choose **Promote to Layer**. The layer's name changes from "Background" to "Layer <number>." To convert a standard layer to a Background layer, right-click the layer and choose **Layer to Background**.

- To convert the layer to a non-destructive filter layer, for applying and managing effect and adjustment filters, right-click and select **Convert to Filter Layer**.

- To access Layer Properties—including Name, Blend Mode, Opacity, and Blend Ranges—right-click the layer name and choose **Properties**.

To control layer content:

- To select all layer content use **Select>Select All** or **Ctrl+A**. To select non-transparent regions on a layer, **Ctrl**-click on a layer thumbnail. Use **Select>Invert** or **Ctrl+Shift+I** to select transparent regions.

-  To move layer content, select one or more layers containing the content to be moved (from the Layers tab), then drag with the **Move Tool** with no selection area present (press **Ctrl+D** to remove any selection).

- To align layer content, select multiple layers (as above), then choose **Align** from the **Layers** menu, then select an option from the submenu.

Adjusting opacity/transparency

Opacity and **transparency** describe essentially the same thing. They both describe the extent to which a particular pixel's colour contributes to the overall colour at that point in the image. Fully opaque pixels contribute their full colour value to the image. Fully transparent pixels are invisible: they contribute nothing to the image. In-between pixels are called semi-transparent.

| *Fully opaque text* | *Semi-transparent text* |
| *(100% Opacity)* | *(50% Opacity)* |

You'll primarily encounter opacity in one of these two contexts:

- As a property of the pixels laid down by individual **tools** (Paintbrush, Clone, Eraser, Fill, Smudge, QuickShape, and more).

- As a property of individual **standard layers**. The layer's opacity setting affects all the pixels on the layer, and is cumulative with the opacity of individual pixels already there.

To set a tool's opacity:

- Select the tool (e.g., Paintbrush Tool) and from the context toolbar either enter a percentage **Opacity** value directly or use the slider (click the option's right arrow button).

To set a layer's opacity:

- Select the layer in the Layers tab and adjust the **Opacity** setting at the top of the tab—either enter a percentage **Opacity** value directly or use the slider (click the option's right arrow button).

To read the opacity values of pixels on all visible layers:

1. Select the ✐ **Colour Pickup Tool** from the **Tools** toolbar and move it around the image.

2. Read the value shown for "O" (Opacity) on the Hintline (e.g., O:60%).

   RGB: 67 255 94 O:60%

   The readout updates constantly, showing the opacity value of each pixel under the cursor.

For more useful hints and tips about using opacity, see PhotoPlus Help.

Using masks

Masking can also be applied to adjustment and effect filters, where you can isolate regions (e.g., an image background) to which you want a filter to be applied. Similarly, you can use studio-based filter masking in PhotoFix (for adjustments) and Warp Studio (for warps).

Creating the mask

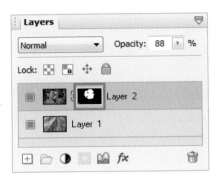

Before you can use a mask, you have to create it on a particular layer. The mask can start out as transparent (revealing the whole layer), opaque (hiding the whole layer), or—if you create it from a selection (opposite)— a bit of both.

The choice depends on how you want to work with the layer's contents. By darkening portions of a clear mask, you can selectively fade layer pixels. By lightening an opaque mask, you selectively reveal layer pixels.

To create a mask:

1. Select a layer in the **Layers tab**. This is the layer where you want to create the mask, and select specific region(s) if desired.

2. Click the **Add Layer Mask** button to create a Reveal All mask (or Reveal Selection if there is one). Instead, **Alt**-click the button for a Hide All Mask (or Hide Selection).

On the Layers tab, a mask preview thumbnail appears, confirming that a mask exists.

Editing on the mask

When you create your mask you immediately enter Edit Mask mode,
where you can use the full range of painting tools, selection options,
flood fills, gradient fills, and effects to alter the mask's greyscale values.
These manipulations cause corresponding changes in opacity, which in
turn changes the appearance of the pixels on the layer itself.

The image window's title bar shows "**Mask**", indicating that a mask is
currently being edited. The Colour tab switches to Greyscale mode when
you're editing a mask, and reverts to the previous setting when you exit
Edit Mask mode. This means anything you paste from the Clipboard
onto the mask will automatically be converted to greyscale.

 As long as you are editing the mask, you're only seeing a preview of changes
on the layer.

You can switch out of Edit Mask mode at any time to edit the active
layer directly (or any other part of the image), then switch back to
resume work on the mask.

To edit the active layer:

- Click the layer thumbnail to the left of the Mask thumbnail.
  The thumbnail is then bordered in white.

To edit the active layer's mask:

- Click the mask thumbnail.

Masks and selections

Once you've created and manipulated a selection, it's easy to turn it into a mask.

To create a mask, revealing the selection:

1. Create a selection (See Making a selection on p. 67).

2. From the **Layers** tab, click 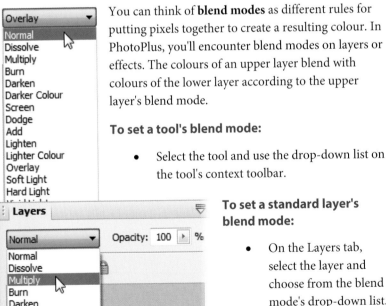 **Add Layer Mask**.

Using blend modes

You can think of **blend modes** as different rules for putting pixels together to create a resulting colour. In PhotoPlus, you'll encounter blend modes on layers or effects. The colours of an upper layer blend with colours of the lower layer according to the upper layer's blend mode.

To set a tool's blend mode:

- Select the tool and use the drop-down list on the tool's context toolbar.

To set a standard layer's blend mode:

- On the Layers tab, select the layer and choose from the blend mode's drop-down list.

Making Image Adjustments

4

Introduction to image adjustments

A major part of photo-editing is making corrections (i.e., **adjustments**) to your own near-perfect images. Whether you've been snapping with your digital camera or you've just scanned a photograph, at some point you may need to call on PhotoPlus's powerful photo-correction tools to fix some unforeseen problems.

For photo-correction, several methods can be adopted. You can use a combination of:

- **Image colour adjustments**: For applying colour adjustments to a selection or layers.

- **PhotoFix**: For making cumulative corrective adjustments from within a studio environment.

- **Retouch** brush-based tools: Red Eye, Smudge, Blur, Sharpen, Dodge/Burn (for exposure control), Sponge (for saturation control), Scratch Remover.

If you work with raw images you can make image adjustments on your unprocessed raw file (before interpolation). See Adjusting raw images on p. 41.

Overview: Adjusting image colours

PhotoPlus provides a number of different adjustment filters that you can apply to a selection or to an active standard layer. Typically, these adjustments are used to correct deficiencies in the original image.

The adjustment can be applied in one of several ways:

- via the **Adjustments tab**, as an **adjustment layer** (non-destructive).

- via **PhotoFix**, a studio environment for managing and applying cumulative adjustments (non-destructive).

- via **Image>Adjust**, on a filter layer (non-destructive).

- via **Image>Adjust**, on a standard layer (destructive).

Here's a summary of the available PhotoPlus image adjustments.

- **Levels**: Displays a histogram plot of lightness values in the image, from which you can adjust the tonal range by shifting dark, light, and gamma values.

- **Curves**: Displays lightness values in the image using a line graph, and lets you adjust points along the curve to fine-tune the tonal range.

- **Brightness/Contrast**: Brightness refers to overall lightness or darkness, while contrast describes the tonal range, or spread between lightest and darkest values.

- **Shadow/Highlight/Midtone**: Controls the extent of shadows, highlights, and contrast within the image.

- **Hue/Saturation**: Hue refers to the colour's tint—what most of us think of as rainbow or spectrum colours with name associations, like "blue" or "magenta". Saturation describes the colour's purity—a totally unsaturated image has only greys. Lightness is what we intuitively understand as relative darkness or lightness—ranging from full black at one end to full white at the other.

- **Colourize**: Lets you recolour an image using Hue, Saturation, and Lightness.

- **Vibrance**: Boosts low-saturation colours in your image, while high-saturation colours are less affected.

- **Colour Balance**: Lets you adjust colour and tonal balance for general colour correction in the image.

- **Replace Colour**: Tags one or more ranges of the full colour spectrum that require adjustment in the image, then apply variations in hue, saturation, and/or brightness to just those colour regions (not to be confused with the simpler Replace Colour Tool).

- **Selective Colour**: Lets you add or subtract a certain percentage of cyan, magenta, yellow, and/or black ink for creating effects.

- **Channel Mixer**: Modifies a colour channel using a mix of the current colour channels.

- **Gradient Map**: Lets you remap greyscale (lightness) information in the image to a selected gradient.

- **Lens Filter**: Adjusts the colour balance for warming or cooling down your photos. It digitally mimics the placement of a filter on the front of your camera lens.

- **Black and White**: Used for greyscale conversion with controllable source channel input.

- **Threshold**: Creates a monochromatic (black and white) rendering. You can set the threshold, i.e. the lightness or grey value above which colours are inverted.

- **Equalize**: Evenly distributes the lightness levels between existing bottom (darkest) and top (lightest) values.

- **Invert**: Inverts the colours, giving the effect of a photographic negative.

- **Clarity**: Lets you sharpen up your photos using local contrast.

- **Posterize**: Produces a special effect by reducing the image to a limited number of colours.

Instead of the manual tonal adjustments above, the PhotoPlus **Image** menu lets you correct shadow/highlight values in an image automatically. **Adjust>AutoLevels** or **Adjust>AutoContrast** may do the job in one go; if not, you can use **Adjust>Levels** or **Adjust>Shadow/Highlight/Midtone**. (See PhotoPlus Help for details.)

 Use the Histogram tab to display statistics and image colour values, helping you to evaluate the kinds of image adjustments that may be needed.

Using adjustment layers

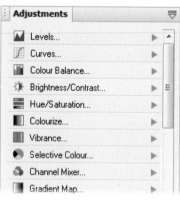

Adjustment layers are recommended for applying image adjustments experimentally and non-destructively to your image.

An adjustment layer is created by selecting an adjustment from the **Adjustments tab**. As its name suggests, an adjustment layer is considered a layer so it will appear in the Layers tab on creation.

The Adjustments tab lists available adjustments in a selectable adjustments list. After selection, the tab displays a Settings pane for that adjustment (and for any selected adjustment layer present in the Layers tab).

Unlike the other layer types, adjustment layers don't store content in the form of bitmap images, text, or shapes. Rather, an adjustment layer applies the adjustment to content on **all** layers below it (although you can restrict the effects of the adjustment by adding to a group or by clipping to the immediate layer below).

The layer is essentially a container in which only the adjustment's settings and its layer properties are stored.

Adjustment layers let you revisit the settings for a given adjustment as often as needed, while continuing to edit the image in other ways. If you later decide you don't even need an adjustment, you can simply remove it!

For more in-depth details on each adjustment, view the PhotoPlus help, click the Contents tab, and open the *Making Image Adjustments* book.

To create an adjustment layer:

1. From the **Adjustments** tab, select an adjustment. You can choose a default adjustment or a named preset by expanding the adjustment entry (click).

2. In the **Layers** tab, the new adjustment layer is inserted above the active layer. The adjustment is applied to all underlying layers.

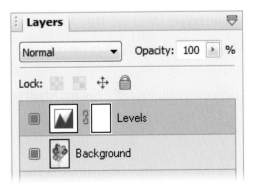

3.   From the **Adjustments** tab, change the applied adjustment layer's settings to suit your requirements. For example, for a levels adjustment, you can drag the histogram pointers to alter levels.

To save an adjustment layer as a new preset:

1.   Select and then modify an adjustment layer in the **Adjustments** tab.

2.   Click ⊞ **Add Preset**.

3.   From the dialog, name your custom adjustment layer, and click **OK**.

Custom adjustments will appear under the adjustment's type in the tab's adjustment list.

To modify an adjustment layer:

1.   Click the adjustment layer's name in the **Layers** tab.

2.   From the Adjustments tab, modify the applied adjustment layer's settings.

To hide/show an adjustment layer:

*   Click **Hide/Show Layer** on the **Layers** tab.

To reset an adjustment layer:

1.   Click the adjustment layer's name in the **Layers** tab.

2.   From the Adjustments tab, select ⟲ **Restore Default Settings**.

Adjusting raw images

PhotoPlus's **Import Raw** dialog offers post-shoot adjustments to your raw file **without** affecting the original file. **White balance**, **exposure**, **highlight recovery**, **noise reduction**, and the removal of **chromatic aberration** are all possible. With an in-built histogram, it's easy to firstly check exposure levels and to spot any highlight clipping (suggesting image overexposure), and to secondly make adjustments using the human eye and the histogram in combination.

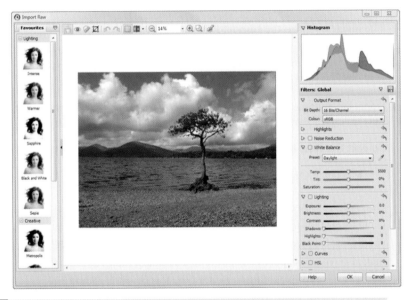

Opening 16-bit HD photos will automatically adopt a 16-bits/channel Colour mode to maintain high-quality colour or tonal detail.

To open a raw image:

1. Open PhotoPlus to display the initial Startup Assistant.

   - or -

   Select **Startup Assistant** from the **File** menu (during your session).

2. Select **Open**.

3. In the Open dialog, select the folder and file name. To open multiple files, press the **Shift** or **Ctrl** key when selecting their names (for adjacent or non-adjacent files).

4. Click **Open**.

   - or -

• Drag and drop a raw file into PhotoPlus from Windows Explorer.

The image opens in the **Import Raw** dialog.

Import Raw performs some preprocessing to attempt to correct the levels on your photo. However, you may wish to make further, manual adjustments.

If opening multiple raw files, once you've adjusted the first image, the **Import Raw** dialog will load the next image automatically until all files are loaded.

To exit the Raw Image dialog:

• Click **OK**.

Once you've exited the Import Raw dialog, you photo will display in the usual PhotoPlus user interface. On saving (**File>Save** or **File>Save As**), you'll be prompted to save your work as a PhotoPlus picture (SPP). You may also wish to export your photo to a standard image format. (See Saving a file and Exporting to another file format on p. 19 and 113, respectively, for more information.)

Using the Import Raw dialog

The filters on the right of the dialog allow you to make common adjustments to your photo including white balance, lighting, highlight recovery, noise reduction, and removal of chromatic aberration.

To enable any filter:

- Click ☐ **Enable** in the filter's title bar.

If needed, expand a filter to display its settings, by clicking the ▷ **Expand/Collapse filter**.

To set output format:

- On the **Output Format** section:

  - (Optional) From the **Bit Depth** drop-down list, select **8 Bits/Channel** to reduce the colour information within the image output.

    By default, optimum raw colour information is preserved (i.e., 16 Bits/Channel).

  - (Optional) From the **Colour Space** drop-down list, assign a colour space to your image which matches your intended colour **workspace**.

    For professional work, AdobeRGB, ProPhoto, or WideGamut offer larger colour spaces (i.e more colours) than the standard RGB (sRGB) space (this is acceptable for most users), but you'll need to enable colour management and pick the same colour space as your chosen workspace.

Most of the adjustments you can make to your photo in the Import Raw dialog are also available in PhotoFix. For more information, see Using PhotoFix on p. 46.

Lens correction

PhotoPlus lets you correct a range of lens distortions in your images within a single studio. Combinations of lens and tilt corrections can be made, along with a powerful image straightening.

To open the Lens Correction studio:

- With an image already open, select **Lens Correction** from the **Effects** menu.

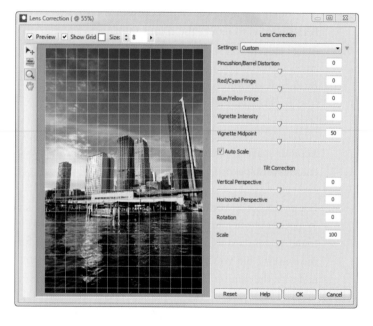

You can carry out the following actions using various tools in the studio:

- **View (and Move) a Grid**: A customizable visual overlay to help you spot and correct distortion.

- **Straightening**: use a horizon line to quickly straighten images.

- **Zoom**: Click and drag over your image to focus on an area in more detail. Shift-click to zoom out.

- **Pan**: Shift the view to navigate around a zoomed-in image.

Apply the following from the Lens Correction section:

- **Pincushion/Barrel Distortion**: Most commonly used to fix images that have a slight bulge due to lens flaws.

- **Red/Cyan** and **Blue/Yellow Fringe**: Correct colour halos sometimes found in areas of high contrast.

- **Vignette Intensity** and **Vignette Midpoint**: Compensate for darkness at the corners of images.

- **Autoscale** zooms the image to trim away transparent edges introduced by lens corrections.

- **Save and Apply Settings**: Quickly reapply your favourite or last-used adjustments to save time and effort.

And using the Tilt Correction section:

- **Vertical Perspective**: Corrects perspective distortion (about the X-axis) caused by camera tilt.

- **Horizontal Perspective**: As for Vertical Perspective but about the Y-axis.

- **Rotation**: Straightens your image if appearing slanted as a result of perspective distortion.

- **Scale**: Simulates a zoomed-in lens, with cropping of your image.

Using PhotoFix

PhotoFix provides an image **adjustment** environment within PhotoPlus which simplifies the often complicated process of image correction.

To launch PhotoFix:

- Click 👁 **PhotoFix** on the **Photo Studio** toolbar.

(A) Retouch tools, (B) Main toolbar, (C) Main Workspace, (D) Histogram, (E) Filters, (F) Favourites.

Adjustments overview

Here's a quick overview of all the adjustments hosted in PhotoFix, some tool-based and some available as filters. The tool-based adjustments are:

Red Eye	Spot Repair	Crop/Straighten

Filter are made available from the **Filters** section.

Noise Reduction	White Balance	Lighting	Curves
HSL	Black and White Film	Chromatic Aberration	Lens Distortion
	Lens Vignette	Unsharp Mask	

You'll also be able to apply adjustments selectively using both standard masking (see p. 48) and gradient masking (see PhotoPlus Help).

To apply an adjustment (from a favourites preset):

1. From the **Favourites tab**, scroll the tab to review the categorized adjustments; select a preset or custom thumbnail.

2. Click **OK**.

When applied, your image layer is **automatically** converted to a non-destructive filter layer with a PhotoFix adjustment entry nested under the filter layer entry.

To apply an adjustment (using custom settings):

1. Review the available adjustments in the Filters section, before expanding the adjustment you want to apply by clicking ▷ **Expand.**

2. Modify the adjustment using sliders, check boxes, graph adjustments, and drop-down lists. The image will be adjusted automatically to reflect the new settings in the preview window. The adjustment filter is enabled once a setting is changed, i.e. the ☐ **Enable/disable filter** option becomes greyed out (▣).

3. Click **OK**. A filter layer is created.

To reset (and disable) a modified adjustment:

- Click ↰ **Reset settings** on the adjustment's pane.

To edit PhotoFix adjustments:

- Double-click the PhotoFix entry on the filter layer.

To apply a standard mask:

1. Select 🖌 **Create mask** from the main toolbar. The Mask entry appears in the Filters section, opened by clicking ▷ **Expand**.

2. (Optional) Adjust the settings in the Mask pane.

3. Using the 🖱 cursor, paint the regions to be masked.

4. (Optional) Click the **Invert** option to invert your mask, i.e. areas that were masked become unmasked (and vice versa).

5. Apply your adjustment from the Filters section, which will make a change to your masked regions.

6. Click on 🖌 **Create mask** again to deactivate masking.

Adding Image Effects

5

Overview: Applying special effects

Special effects such as **distort**, **blur**, **sharpen**, **edge**, **noise**, **render**, **stylistic**, and **artistic** offer you a diverse choice of creative opportunities in PhotoPlus.

Before going ahead and applying your effects, it's a good idea to review Using filter layers (see p. 51) before deciding on your approach, i.e. whether you work non-destructively or destructively.

Each effect can be applied in one of several ways:

- On a filter layer, via an Effects dialog or via the Filter Gallery (non-destructive).

- On a standard layer, via an Effects dialog or via the Filter Gallery (destructive).

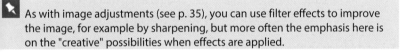

As with image adjustments (see p. 35), you can use filter effects to improve the image, for example by sharpening, but more often the emphasis here is on the "creative" possibilities when effects are applied.

Using filter layers

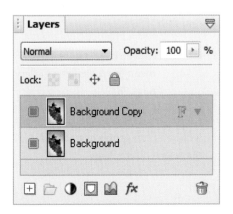

If you apply a filter effect to a standard or background layer, the layer is permanently altered.

However, if you want the flexibility of being able to edit your filters at any point in the future (and don't want to destroy the layer contents) you can **convert** your standard or background layer to a **Filter Layer** (e.g., Background Copy).

When applied, filters are created within **filter groups**, nested individually under the Filter Layer. When you double-click a filter you display its specific settings. You can apply a blend mode and opacity to each filter, and additionally filter masking to the filter group.

 For added security, it's good practice to create a duplicate of any background layer you initially have.

To convert to a filter layer:

- In the Layers tab, right-click a standard or Background layer and choose **Convert to Filter Layer**.

  The layer now shows the letter "F" indicating that it is now a filter layer, and ready to have a filter applied.

To add filters to the filter layer:

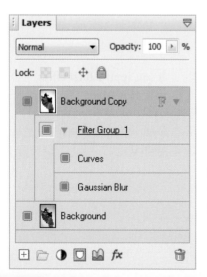

1. Select the filter layer.

2. Add an adjustment via the **Image** menu.
   - or -

   Add an effect via the **Effects** menu or via the Filter Gallery on p. 56.

Each filter, as it is applied, is created within a filter group nested under the selected filter layer.

Editing filters

Once a filter is applied, it's likely that you may want to edit it at a later date.

To edit a filter:

1. Double-click the filter entry, e.g. Gaussian Blur.

2. The filter can then be edited via dialog or Filter Gallery. Adjust the filter and click **OK**.

Using filter masks

In an identical way to layer masks (see p. 29) you can apply a **mask** to a filter layer. However, masks can additionally be used for selective filter control for image correction or artistic reasons. These are called **filter masks**, which limit the influence of any applied filter(s) to that masked region only. Filter masks are applied either automatically (from a selection existing before applying a filter) or manually (after you've applied the filter) to a **filter group** (but never to an individual filter).

See Using masks (see p. 29) for more details on masking and masking controls.

To create a filter mask (from a selection):

1. Make a selection on which your mask will be based, e.g. a brush selection around the subject of interest. By default the area outside the selection is masked (i.e. not affected by the filter), while the selection area retains the applied filter. If you want to do the opposite, choose **Invert** from the **Select** menu.

2. In the Layers tab, select the filter layer to which you wish to apply a filter.

3. Add an adjustment via the **Image** menu.
    - or -

    Add an effect via the **Effects** menu or via the Filter Gallery.

    The filter is created within an automatically created filter group, which applies a mask automatically.

4. (Optional) Fine-tune the filter by double-clicking the filter entry and editing the settings.

To create a filter mask (by mask painting):

1. With no selections present, in the Layers tab, select the filter layer to which you wish to apply a filter.

2. Add an adjustment via the **Image** menu.
    - or -

    Add an effect via the **Effects** menu or via the Filter Gallery.

3. Right-click the created filter group and select **Add Mask** from the flyout menu and then one of the following from the submenu:

    - **Reveal All** for a transparent mask

    - **Hide All** for an opaque mask.

    A mask thumbnail appears to the left of the filter name.

4. Paint or draw on your image using a suitable greyscale value set as your foreground colour. The mask thumbnail updates accordingly.

To disable (enable) a mask:

- Right-click the filter group and select **Disable Mask** (or **Enable Mask**) from the flyout menu.

To delete a mask:

- Right-click the filter group and select **Delete Mask** from the flyout menu.

Using the Filter Gallery

The Filter Gallery offers a one-stop studio environment for applying **single** or **multiple** filter effects. The gallery hosts sets of filter thumbnails which are categorized into different effect categories (e.g., Distort, Blur, Sharpen, Edge, Artistic, Noise, Render, etc.).

The Filter Gallery offers the following key features:

- Application of individual or multiple filter effects simultaneously.

- Preview window with zoom and pan support.

- Optional **Before** and **After** views arranged as tiles or split-screen, both horizontally and vertically.

- Apply filters permanently to a standard layer or on a Filter Layer (see p. 51). The latter allows you to protect your image layer, as well as manage your filters at a later date.

To view the Filter Gallery:

- Click  **Filter Gallery** on the Photo Studio toolbar.

For some effects hosted on the **Effects** menu, the Filter Gallery will automatically be launched with the effect already applied.

To add a filter in the Filter Gallery:

1. Expand your chosen effect category by clicking the ⊞ **Expand** button (click ⊟ to collapse).

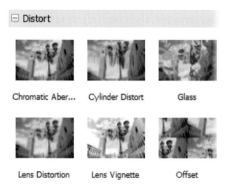

2. Click on an effect thumbnail to apply it to your image.

The applied filter is shown in a **Filters** stack in the lower-right corner of the Filter Gallery. The properties of any selected effect will be displayed in the expanded area under the effect name—you can alter and experiment with these at any time. The filter shows on a light background to indicate selection.

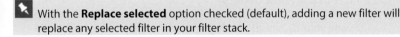 Use the **Undo** button to undo recent changes to the filter (or the **Redo** button to re-apply the changes).

3. Adjust sliders (or enter input values) until your filter suits your requirements.

> With the **Replace selected** option checked (default), adding a new filter will replace any selected filter in your filter stack.

To add multiple filters:

*   Uncheck **Replace selected**, then add one or more additional effects as described above.

Any filter can be temporarily disabled, reset, or deleted once applied.

To disable:	Click ▣, then click ▢ to enable again.
To reset:	Click ↰. Any changes to settings are reverted back to the filter's defaults.
To delete:	Click ✕. The filter is removed from the stack.

The effect's properties are expanded by default but can be collapsed to make more of the Filters stack visible.

To collapse/expand filter properties:

*   To collapse, click the ▽ button preceding the filter effect name. To expand again, click the ▷ button.

To replace a filter:

*   Ensure **Replace selected** is checked.

- Select the filter you wish to replace by clicking anywhere in the filter's pane. On selection, the selected filter shows a lighter background, e.g, Gaussian below.

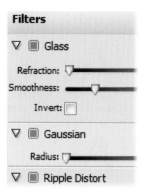

- Select a replacement filter from an effect category. Your selected filter is replaced in the stack with no change made to the existing stack order.

Filters can be moved around the filter list to change the order in which they are applied to the photo.

To reorder filters:

- Drag and drop your filter into any position in the stack. A dotted line indicates the new position in which the entry will be placed on mouse release.

Applying 2D layer effects

Layer effects can be applied to the contents of standard layers, text layers, or shape layers. Standard or "2D" layer effects like shadow, glow, bevel, and emboss are particularly well adapted to text, while 3D layer effects (p. 61) create the impression of a textured surface.

Unlike image adjustments and **Effects** menu manipulations, layer effects don't directly change image pixels—they work like mathematical "lenses" that transform how a layer's bitmap appears. Since the settings are independent, you can adjust them ad infinitum until you get the result you want!

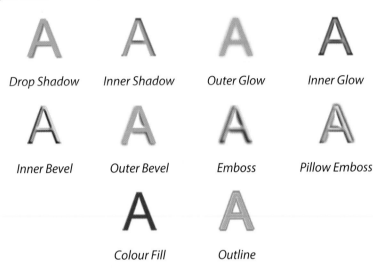

Drop Shadow   Inner Shadow   Outer Glow   Inner Glow

Inner Bevel   Outer Bevel   Emboss   Pillow Emboss

Colour Fill   Outline

To apply a 2D effect:

1. From the Layers tab, select a layer and click *fx* **Add Layer Effects.**.

2. In the dialog, apply an effect by checking its check box in the list at left. You can apply multiple effects to the layer.

3. To adjust the properties of a specific effect, select its name and adjust the dialog controls. Adjust the sliders, drop-down list, or enter specific values to vary each effect. Options differ from one effect to another.

4. Click **OK** to apply the effect or **Cancel** to abandon changes.

Applying 3D layer effects

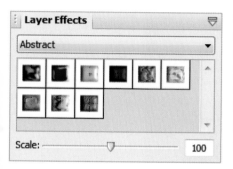

3D layer effects are just as easy to apply, but they're a bit more complex than their 2D cousins (see p. 59). Actually, there's an easy way to get started with them: simply display the **Layer Effects tab**, then select a gallery thumbnail.

If hidden, make this tab visible via **Window>Studio Tabs**.

To apply a layer effect to the active layer:

- From the **Layer Effects** tab, select a category, then click a gallery thumbnail.

- To make the effect smaller or larger, drag the **Scale** slider.

fx If you want to have complete flexibility when creating 3D effects, you can click **Add Layer Effects** on the Layers tab. The dialog is shared for both 2D and 3D effects—simply check the 3D Effects box and enable other 3D check boxes as appropriate.

For more information about creating 3D filter effects, see PhotoPlus Help.

Using Warp Studio

The **Warp Studio** is an exciting feature in PhotoPlus that lets you move your image's pixels around using a variety of brush-based tools. You can deform the image's pixels in equally subtle and dramatic ways, as if your image had a liquid surface.

When you use a warp tool, the actual amount of pixel displacement depends on the direction or amount of brush movement along with the tool's settings, selectable from the top toolbar.

The tools are also supported by a masking feature, which paints protected regions that act as a barrier against warping effects. You can even include already selected regions, layer masks, and layer transparency in Warp Studio. For more subtle warps, a mesh grid can be applied over your image to easily indicate areas of change.

For both features, see PhotoPlus Help for more information.

Warp tool overview

The vertical toolbar on the left of the Warp Studio offers all your warping tools.

The  **Elastic Warp Tool** shifts pixels in the direction of brush motion, hence the appearance of pulling or elasticity. Drag across the image to shift pixels in the direction of brush motion. Compare the original (left) and the warped image (right).

The **Pinch** and **Punch Tools** apply, respectively, a concave or convex spherical distortion under the brush. Click and drag in the region you want to change.

The **Twirl Tools** produce a "spin art" effect—liquid paint on a surface revolving either clockwise or anti-clockwise around a central point. Click and drag in the region you want to change.

The  **Push Left Warp Tool** shifts pixels 90° to the left of the brush direction, which has the effect of spreading or compressing edges along the stroke.

Creating warp effects

To launch Warp Studio:

1. Select an image to be warped.

2. Select **Warp Studio** from the **Photo Studio** toolbar. Warp Studio is launched.

3. Select a warp tool from the left-hand toolbar.

4. (Optional) Select a preset brush from the **Brushes** tab at the right of the studio.

5. Change brush properties, if necessary, on the toolbar above the studio workspace.

6. Paint across your image to apply the chosen warp.

7. Click **OK**.

Manipulating Images

6

Making a selection

In any photo editing program, the **selection tools and techniques** are as significant as any of the basic brush tools or commands. The basic principle is simple: quite often you'll want to perform an operation on just a portion of the image. To do this you must define an active selection area.

The wide range of selection options in PhotoPlus lets you:

- Define just about any selection shape, using various drawing and painting techniques.

- Modify the extent or properties of the selection

- Carry out various manipulations on the selected pixels, including cut, copy, paste, rotate, adjust colours, apply special effects, etc.

Selection basics

Although the techniques for using the various selection methods differ, the end result is always the same: a portion of the active layer has been "roped off" from the rest of the image. The boundary is visible as a broken line or **marquee** around the selected region (see above).

Whenever there's a selection, certain tools and commands operate **only** on the pixels inside the selection—as opposed to a condition where nothing is selected, in which case those functions generally affect the entire active layer.

To cancel the selection (select nothing):

- From the **Select** menu, click **Deselect** (or press **Ctrl+D**)

Selection tool options

PhotoPlus offers a very wide range of other selection methods, and a variety of commands for modifying the extent or properties of the selected pixels—all available from the Tools toolbar. Note that the selection tools work on Background and standard layers, but not on text layers or shape layers.

Available from:	Tools
Selection Tools flyout	**Rectangle Selection Tool**—drag out a rectangular selection area of your chosen size (use the **Ctrl** key to constrain to a square area).
	Ellipse Selection Tool—drag out an ellipse selection area (use **Ctrl** key to constrain to a circle).
	QuickShape Selection Tools flyout—provides different variable shapes, including pie, star, arrow, heart, spiral, wave, and so on. The shapes can be further "morphed" into other custom QuickShapes by dragging node handles around the QuickShape.
Lasso Tools flyout	**Freehand Selection Tool**—lets you draw a freehand (irregular) line which is closed automatically to create an irregularly shaped selection area.

Polygon Selection Tool—lets you draw a series of straight-line segments (double-click to close the polygon).

Magnetic Selection Tool—lets you trace around an object edge creating a selection line that snaps to the edge as you drag.

Directly from toolbar

Magic Wand Tool—lets you select a region based on the colour similarity of adjacent pixels—simply click a starting pixel, setting a **Tolerance** from the context toolbar. It works much like the fill tool, but the result is a selected region rather than a region flooded with a colour. (For a dialog-based selection method, use the **Colour Range** command as detailed below.)

Smart Selection Brush—lets you create your selection as a series of brush strokes.

From the **Select** menu

Paint to Select mode—lets you use standard painting or editing tools as selection tools.

T ▾ Text Tools flyout

Text Selection Tool—lets you create a selection in the form of text. Click with the tool to display the Text cursor. Type your text, format as needed, and click **OK**. (See Creating and editing text on p. 98.)

For any selection tool, the Context toolbar includes combination buttons (**New**, **Add**, **Subtract**, and **Intersect**) that determine the effect of each new selection operation.

Changing image and canvas size

You probably know that image dimensions are given in **pixels** ("dots of paint" that comprise a screen image). In PhotoPlus there are options to change the **image size** and to change the **canvas size**, but what's the difference and how do you perform each resize?

Changing image size

Changing the image size means scaling the whole image (or just a selected region) up or down. Resizing is actually a kind of distortion because the image content is being stretched or squashed.

The Image Size dialog lets you specify a new size for the whole image, in terms of its screen dimensions and/or printed dimensions.

To resize the image for on-screen display:

1.   From the **Image** menu, select **Image Size**.

2. Select a preferred scale (either "pixels" or "percent") in the drop-down list.

3. Select a **Resampling method**. As a rule, use **Nearest Pixel** for hard-edge images, **Bilinear Interpolation** when shrinking photos, **Bicubic Interpolation** when enlarging photos, and **Lanczos3 Window** when best quality results are expected.

4. Enter new **Width**, **Height** or **Resolution** values.

5. Click **OK**.

To resize the image for print:

1. From the **Image** menu, select **Image Size**.

2. Uncheck **Resize layers**.

3. Enter new **Width**, **Height** or **Resolution** values.

4. Click **OK**.

Changing canvas size

Changing the canvas size just involves adding or taking away pixels around the edges of the image. It's like adding to the neutral border around a mounted photo, or taking a pair of scissors and cropping the photo to a smaller size. In either case, the remaining image pixels are undisturbed so there's no distortion.

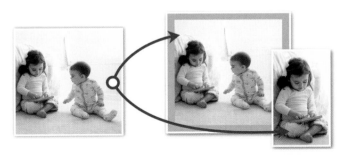

You will change the canvas size when:

- you want to add a border to your image (without changing the size of the image itself).

- you crop an image.

To change canvas size:

1. From the **Image** menu, select **Canvas Size**.

2. Enter **New Width** and/or **New Height** values (the current values are also shown for comparison).

3. In the Anchor box, click to position the image thumbnail with respect to edges where pixels should be added or subtracted.

4. Click **OK**.

If you want to extend the canvas from all sides of the image, click the centre anchor point.

If the canvas size is increased, the new canvas area is filled (on the Background layer) with the current background colour and (on standard layers) with transparency.

Straightening photos

As an image adjustment, the **Straighten Tool** can be used to align a crooked image back to horizontal (e.g., restoring proper horizontal alignment in a scanned image that wasn't aligned correctly on the scanner). Use the tool to trace a new horizon against a line in the image—the image automatically orients itself to the drawn horizon.

Before   *After*
(horizon line drawn by dragging)

You can straighten using one of two methods: As a separate tool used directly on your image (below) (destructive) or via the PhotoFix (non-destructive) studio environment (see p. 46).

To straighten (via Straighten Tool):

1. On the **Tools** Toolbar, expand the ⬚ ▾ **Crop Tools** flyout and click the ▧ **Straighten Tool**.

2. On the context toolbar, choose an option from the **Canvas** drop-down list. This lets you decide how your straightened image will be displayed:

    - **Crop** - Crops and adjusts the straightened image so that it displays on the largest possible canvas size, without displaying any border.

- **Expand to Fit** - Increases the canvas size to display the entire straightened image. The border area is filled with the current background colour.

- **Original Size** - Displays the straightened image within the original canvas dimensions. The border area is filled with the current background colour.

On the image that needs straightening, look for a straight line on the image to which you can set the new horizon (e.g., the divide between the land and sky above).

3. (Optional) Uncheck **Rotate All Layers** to restrict the operation to the active layer only. Otherwise all layers are rotated.

4. Using the Straighten cursor, drag a horizon from one end of the image's line to the other (the length of the horizon is not important) then release. The image orients itself to the new line.

Cropping an image

Cropping is the electronic equivalent of taking a pair of scissors to a photograph, except of course with a pair of scissors there is no second chance! Cropping deletes all of the pixels outside the crop selection area, and then resizes the image canvas so that only the area inside the crop selection remains. Use it to focus on an area of interest—either for practical reasons or to improve photo composition.

You can crop larger areas when photos are shot at a high resolution. Keep this in mind before taking photos and make sure your camera is set to its highest image quality.

Using the Crop Tool

Before

After
(Rectangular Crop)

PhotoPlus allows you to crop unconstrained, or to a standard or custom print size.

To crop unconstrained:

1. From the Tools toolbar's **Crop Tools** flyout, select the **Crop Tool**. Ensure the **Unconstrained** option is set in the Context toolbar's first drop-down list.

2. Drag out a rectangle to create an unconstrained rectangle, then fine-tune the areas dimensions if needed by dragging the edges.

3. To crop to the designated size, double-click inside the crop area.

Cropping with the Crop Tool affects all image layers. Everything outside the designated region is eliminated. If there's a marquee-based selection, it is ignored and deselected during cropping.

To crop to a specific print size or resolution:

1. Select the  **Crop Tool** from the Tools toolbar.

2. Then either:

    - For print sizes, choose a **pre-defined** print size (expressed in inches or centimetres) from the first drop-down list in the Context toolbar.

      - or -

    - If you need to set a **custom** size, enter values into the Height and Width drop-down lists.

3. Drag out your crop area to create your constrained rectangle or square (if Custom).

4. Double-click the crop area to crop to the designated size.

To undo a non-destructive crop:

- From the **Image** menu, click **Reveal All**.

Using rule of thirds

Use the **Thirds grid** check box on the Context toolbar for improving photo composition. A grid is superimposed on top of your photo when the check box is selected.

Moving and resizing the grid allows the main subject of your photo to be offset within the photo.

Position a main item of interest in the photo where any two lines intersect within the crop grid (four intersections are possible). This is known as the "rule of thirds" which will help you find the most balanced composition where your eyes are drawn to the main subject.

Double-click to crop the photo to the outer grid dimensions.

Cropping to a selection

You can also crop an image to any **selection area**, no matter what shape, as defined with one of the selection tools.

If the Rectangle or Ellipse Selection Tool is used, you can make your selection a **Fixed Size**, defined in pixels, from the tool's Context toolbar. This **crop to pixel** operation is heavily used when creating precisely dimensioned web graphics or specific ebook cover dimensions.

To crop the image to the selection:

1. Make your selection.

2. Choose **Crop to Selection** from the **Image** menu.

Flipping and rotating

Flipping and rotating are standard manipulations that you can carry out on the whole image, the active layer, a path, or just on a selection. Flips are used to change the direction of a subject's gaze, fix composition, and so on, whereas rotation is an orientation tool for general purpose use.

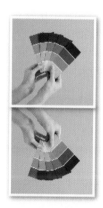

Flip Horizontal

Flip Vertical

*Rotate
15° anti-clockwise*

*Rotate
10° clockwise*

To flip:

1. From the **Image** menu, select either **Flip Horizontally** or **Flip Vertically**.

2. Choose **Image**, **Layer**, **Selection** or **Path** from the submenu.

To rotate:

1. From the **Image** menu, select **Rotate**.

2.   From the flyout menu, select an option based on the object (Image, Layer, or Selection), rotation angle (90° or 180°), and the direction (Clockwise or Anti-clockwise) required.

3.   You can also select **Custom**, to display a **Rotate** dialog, from which you can do all of the above but instead set your own custom angle, even down to fractional degrees.

Using Cutout Studio

Cutout Studio offers a powerful integrated solution for cutting out part of an image on an active Background or standard layer. In doing so, you can separate subjects of interest from their backgrounds, either by retaining the subject of interest (usually people, objects, etc.) or removing a simple uniform background (e.g., sky, studio backdrop). In both instances, the resulting "cutout" creates an eye-catching look for your image, and lets you present cutouts layer-by-layer—great for simulating subject/background combinations and artistic collages.

A checkerboard pattern on the second image's background on preview is used to indicate areas to be discarded.

To launch Cutout Studio:

1.   Select an image to be cut out.

2.   Select **Cutout Studio** from the Photo Studio toolbar.

Selecting areas to keep or discard

A pair of brushes for keeping and discarding is used to "paint" areas on your active layer. The tools are called **Keep Brush** and **Discard Brush**, and are either used independently or, more typically, in combination with each other.

To select areas for keeping/discarding:

1.   In Cutout Studio, click either **Keep Brush Tool** or **Discard Brush Tool** from the left of the Studio workspace.

2.   (Optional) Pick a **Brush size** suitable for the area to be worked on.

3.   (Optional) Set a **Grow tolerance** value to automatically expand the selected area under the cursor (by detecting colours similar to those within the current selection). The greater the value the more the selected area will grow.

4.   Using the circular cursor, click and drag across the area to be retained or discarded (depending on Keep or Discard Brush Tool selection).

     The **Undo** button reverts to the last made selection.

5.   Click **OK** to create your cutout.

Painting, Drawing and Text

Painting and brushes

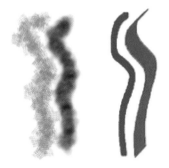

The 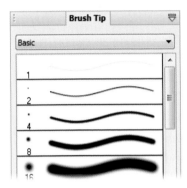 **Paintbrush Tool** and **Pencil Tool** on the Tools toolbar are the basic tools for painting and drawing freehand lines on the active layer. They work on Background and standard layers, but not on text layers or shape layers.

The **Brush Tip tab** hosts a comprehensive collection of brush presets grouped into various categories. Note that each sample clearly shows the brush tip and stroke; the number indicates the brush diameter.

You can also create your own brush from within the tab.

If a more bespoke brush tip is required, you can also customize your own brush tip and save it in its own user-defined category. (See Creating your own brush tips in PhotoPlus Help for details.)

To use the Paintbrush or Pencil tool:

1.   From the **Tools** toolbar's **Brush Tools** flyout, select the **Paintbrush Tool** or **Pencil Tool**.

2.   Choose a brush tip preset on the **Brush Tip** tab. If you've picked a Basic brush, set a brush colour (i.e. the foreground colour) from the Colour tab before painting.

3. (Optional) Change the brush tip's attributes, if necessary, on the Context toolbar.

4. Drag the cursor on the active layer, holding the left mouse button down to paint in the foreground colour.

Brush options

The Brush Options dialog, accessible by double-clicking the brush sample on the context toolbar, lets you customize a brush or define properties for a new one. As you vary the settings, you can see the effect of each change in the preview window at the bottom of the dialog.

 Available settings may vary, depending on the brush you've got selected.

Painting using pen tablets

Brush strokes can be applied directly to the page by using your mouse or, if available, a pen tablet; the latter method is ideally suited for applying pressure-sensitive strokes to your project. PhotoPlus supports pressure sensitivity, with tablet calibration and key assignment possible directly from within the program (via Pressure Studio).

Erasing

Sometimes the rubber end of the pencil can be just as important to an artist as the pointed one. The Eraser Tools flyout on the Tools toolbar provides ways of enhancing an image by "painting" with transparency rather than with colour.

 Use the **Standard Eraser** for replacing colours in an image either with the background colour or with transparency (on Background or other standard layers, respectively).

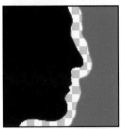 Use the **Background Eraser** for erasing pixels similar to a sampled reference colour underlying the cursor crosshair—great for painting out unwanted background colours.

 Use the **Flood Eraser** for filling a region with transparency, erasing pixels similar to the colour under the cursor when you first click.

In general, you can set tool properties for each tool including brush characteristics, opacity, tolerance, flow, and choose a brush tip. The Eraser tools work on Background and standard layers, but not on text layers or shape layers.

To erase with the Standard Eraser:

1. Select ![icon] **Standard Eraser** from the **Tools** toolbar's **Eraser Tools** flyout.

2. (Optional) Change attributes, especially brush **Size** and **Opacity**, on the Context toolbar.

For erasing with an airbrush effect or hard-edged brush, check the **Airbrush** or **Hard Edge** option.

For tablet users, pressure sensitivity can be switched on via Brush Options (click **Brush** thumbnail); ensure the **Controller** drop-down list is set to "Pressure" on selected attributes.

3.   Drag with the tool on the active layer. On the Background layer, erased pixels expose the current background colour. On other layers, they expose transparency.

To erase with the Background Eraser:

1.   Select ![] **Background Eraser** from the **Tools** toolbar's **Eraser Tools** flyout.

2.   (Optional) Change properties on the Context toolbar:

- For tablet users, pressure sensitivity can be switched on via Brush Options (click **Brush** thumbnail); ensure the **Controller** drop-down list is set to "Pressure" on selected attributes.

- The **Tolerance** setting determines the breadth of the colour range to be erased.

- You also have the option of protecting the current foreground colour from erasure (**Protect foreground**).

3.   Drag with the tool on the active layer to erase pixels similar to a sampled reference colour directly under the brush tip.

 If you use the tool on the Background layer, it's promoted to a standard layer.

To erase with the Flood Eraser:

1.   Select ![] **Flood Eraser** from the **Tools** toolbar's **Eraser Tools** flyout.

2.   (Optional) Change properties on the Context toolbar.

3.   Click (or click and drag) with the tool on the active layer to erase pixels close in colour (based on the Tolerance range) to the colour under the cursor when you first click. If you use the tool on the Background layer, it's promoted to a standard layer.

Erasing using pen tablets

For tablet users, PhotoPlus supports pressure sensitivity, with tablet calibration and key assignment possible directly from within the program (via Pressure Studio).

Filling a region

Filling regions or layers is an alternative to brushing on colours or patterns. Making a selection prior to applying a fill, and setting appropriate options, can spell the difference between a humdrum effect and a spectacular one.

The **Fill Tools** flyout on the Tools toolbar includes two tools for filling regions with colour and/or transparency: **Flood Fill** and **Gradient Fill**. In addition, you can use the **Edit>Fill** command to apply either a **colour** or **pattern** fill. As with paint tools, if there is a selection, the Fill tools only affect pixels within the selected region. If you're operating on a shape or text layer, the **Gradient Fill** tool can be used to adjust the interior of the object(s) on the layer.

Flood and pattern fills

The 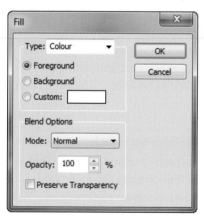 **Flood Fill Tool** works on Background and standard layers, replacing an existing colour region with the foreground colour..

To use the Flood Fill Tool:

1. Select the **Flood Fill Tool** from the **Tools** toolbar's **Fill Tools** flyout.

2. Set tolerance and layer fill options on the context toolbar.

3. Click with the tool where you want to start the fill.

The **Edit>Fill** command lets you flood-fill a region on a standard layer using any colour, not just the foreground colour.

To use the Fill command:

*   From the **Edit** menu, select **Fill**. The Fill dialog appears.

*   For a flood fill, set the **Type** to Colour.

*   Choose whether the fill colour is to be the current **Foreground** colour, **Background** colour or a **Custom** colour.

- Specify the blend mode and opacity of the fill.
  If you check **Preserve Transparency**, transparent areas will resist the flood colour; otherwise, everything in the selection or layer will be equally washed with the fill.

- For a Pattern fill, set the **Type** to **Pattern** to fill a region with any pattern stored in the Patterns dialog. Click the pattern sample to bring up the gallery of pattern thumbnails.

Gradient Fill Tool

Whereas solid fills use a single colour, all gradient fills in PhotoPlus utilize at least two "key" colours, with a spread of hues in between each key colour, creating a "spectrum" effect. You can fine-tune the actual spread of colour between pairs of key colours. Likewise, a gradient fill in PhotoPlus can have either **solid transparency**—one level of opacity, e.g., 50% or 100%, across its entire range—or **variable transparency**, with at least two "key" opacity levels and a spread of values in between.

The ▭ **Gradient Fill Tool** lets you apply variable colour and/or transparency fills directly to a layer.

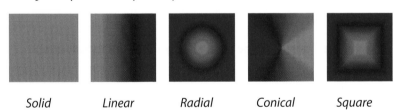

| *Solid* | *Linear* | *Radial* | *Conical* | *Square* |

Applying a gradient fill on any kind of layer entails selecting one of the fill types, editing the fill colours and/or transparency in a Gradient dialog, then applying the fill.

To apply a gradient fill:

1. Select **Gradient Fill Tool** from the **Tools** toolbar's **Fill Tools** flyout.

2. Select a fill type from the context toolbar.

Radial	▾
Linear	
Radial	
Conical	
Square	

3. To choose a preset or to edit the fill's colours and/or transparency values, click the colour sample on the context toolbar.

    The Gradient dialog appears, where you can select a preset fill from the default or a pre-defined gallery (select a category e.g., Natural, Pastels, from the drop-down list).

4. Once you've defined the fill, click with the tool where you want to start the fill and drag to the point where you want it to end.

See PhotoPlus Help for details on how to edit gradient fills.

To change a text or shape layer's fill type, or edit its colour(s):

*   Double-click the text/shape layer.
    - or -

*   Choose the **Gradient Fill Tool** and use the context toolbar.

Either option lets you choose a fill type, and/or click the colour (or gradient) sample to edit the fill.

Cloning a region

When retouching you can remove unwanted objects from an image by extending another area of the image over it. This is possible using the **Clone Tool** which acts like two magic brushes locked together. While you trace or "pick up" an image region with one brush, the other draws ("puts down") an exact duplicate somewhere else even in another image.

For corrective work, you can pick up wanted pixels and put them down over unwanted pixels.

A canal scene spoilt by power cables and pylons

The same scene with unwanted objects cloned out

The tool acts on the active Background or standard layer, and can even clone **all** layers (including Text layers or Shape layers).

To clone a region:

1. From the **Tools** toolbar's **Clone Tools** flyout, select the **Clone Tool**.

2. Change properties, if necessary, on the Context toolbar.

3. To define the pickup origin, **Alt**-click with the tool.

4. Click again where you want to start the copy, then click to paint the copy onto the new location. Repeat as needed. A crosshair marks the pickup point, which moves relative to your brush movements.

Drawing and editing lines and shapes

For drawing and editing lines and shapes, the **Tools** toolbar includes the following drawing tool flyouts:

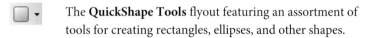 The **QuickShape Tools** flyout featuring an assortment of tools for creating rectangles, ellipses, and other shapes.

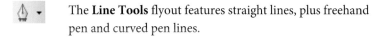 The **Line Tools** flyout features straight lines, plus freehand pen and curved pen lines.

Overview

Each of the drawing tools has its own creation and editing rules, as detailed below:

- Unlike painted regions you create on **raster** (bitmap) layers, both QuickShapes and lines are **vector objects** that occupy **shape layers**, marked with an ⓢ symbol on the Layers tab.

- A QuickShape or straight line can be drawn directly as a **shape layer**, **path** or as a filled **bitmap**. Buttons on the Context toolbar allow you to decide how your lines/shapes are to be drawn, i.e.

    Shape Layer—create your QuickShape or line on a new shape layer or add to an existing shape layer.

    Paths—add your shape or line directly as a path rather than as a shape layer. See PhotoPlus Help.

    Fill Bitmaps—creates a filled bitmap of the shape or straight line on any selected raster layer (e.g., the Background layer).

Creating additional shapes

Shape layers can store more than one shape, and it's up to you where additional shapes are created. The context toolbar displays a series of **combination buttons** which determine the layer on which the shape will be placed and the relationship the new shape will have on any existing shapes on the same layer.

New—adds the shape to a new shape layer.

Add—adds the shape to the currently selected layer.

Subtract—removes overlap region when a new shape is added over existing shapes on the currently selected layer. The new shape itself is not included.

Intersect—includes the intersection area only when a new shape is added onto existing selected shapes on the currently selected layer.

Exclude—excludes the intersection area when a new shape is added onto existing selected shapes on the currently selected layer.

You can also alter a shape layer's **Opacity** using the Layers tab.

Creating and editing QuickShapes

QuickShapes in PhotoPlus let you instantly add all kinds of pre-designed shapes to your image, then adjust and vary them using control handles for shape variations!

The **QuickShape Tools** flyout lets you choose from a wide variety of commonly used shapes, including boxes, ovals, arrows, polygons, stars, and more. Each shape has its own built-in "intelligent" properties, which you can use to customize the basic shape.

To create a QuickShape:

1. Click the ⬜ ▾ **QuickShapes** flyout on the **Tools** Toolbar and select a shape from the flyout menu.

2. Ensure ⬚ **Shape Layers** is selected on the context toolbar.

3. If you want to create the shape on its own layer, make sure the ⬛ **New** button on the Context toolbar is selected. If you want to create multiple shapes on the same layer, select one of the other combination buttons on the Context toolbar to specify how the multiple shapes will interact (see p. 93).

4. For shapes on a new layer only, select a foreground colour on the Colour tab for the QuickShape. Multiple shapes on the layer will adopt the layer's current colour.

5. Drag out the shape on the image. It displays as an outline; hold down the **Ctrl** key while drawing to constrain the aspect ratio.

If you switch to the **Node Edit Tool**, you can adjust the shape. The number of displayed "edit" control handles varies according to the shape; for example, the rectangle has just one control, the polygon has two.

 The Node Edit Tool is automatically selected once you draw a QuickShape, to allow you to customize it.

Using the middle Quick Pentagon shape as an example:

- Dragging the top control handle to the right will morph the shape to a hexagon, heptagon, octagon, and so on.

- Dragging the side control handle downwards will rotate the shape anti-clockwise.

To edit a QuickShape:

1. Click its layer name in the Layers tab to select it.

2. From the Node Tools flyout, use either:

   - The ▷ **Node Edit Tool** (**Tools** toolbar) to click on the shape and readjust any of the shape's handles.
   - or -

   - The ⬚ **Shape Edit Tool** to select, move, resize, and deform individual shapes.

     (If you only have one shape on a layer, you can also use the **Move Tool** and **Deform Tool**.) To resize without constraint, you can drag any shape's handle; to constrain the shape's proportions, hold down the **Shift** key while dragging. To deform the shape, drag a node while the **Ctrl** key is pressed.

Creating and editing lines

Lines can be drawn by using dedicated tools from the **Tools** toolbar's Line Tools flyout.

The **Pen Tool** produces complex curves (and shapes) in a highly controlled way.

The **Freehand Pen Tool**, as its name implies, lets you draw freehand lines. PhotoPlus will compose the line with line segments and nodes (each new segment starting from another's end node), which is attached back to the start point to create a closed shape.

The **Line Tool** produces an anti-aliased straight line in PhotoPlus, which is just a very thin shape. The line can be of varying **Weight** (thickness).

Each tool's supporting context toolbar lets you create the line on a shape layer or as a path. The Line Tool can also be used to create a filled bitmap directly. Additionally, combination buttons let you add the line to its own layer (or path), and can also be used to control how the new line interacts with existing shapes on the layer.

To edit a line:

1. Click its layer name to select it for editing.

2. To move, resize, scale, skew, or rotate the line, choose the **Shape Edit Tool**. This deform tool works by manipulation of the bounding box around the line—drag on a corner or edge.

3. To reshape the line, choose the **Node Edit Tool**. The line consists of **line segments** and **nodes** (points where the line segments meet). You can drag one or more individual nodes, or click and drag directly on a line segment.

When you select a node, control handles for the adjacent line segments appear; each segment in the line has a control handle at either end. Any node can be one of several node types: **sharp**, **smooth**, or **symmetric**. Depending on node type, the node's control handles behave a bit differently; the node type determines the slope and curvature of each adjoining segment, and can be chosen from the context toolbar, i.e.

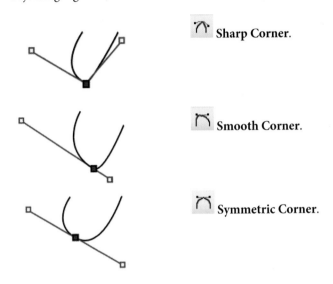

Sharp Corner.

Smooth Corner.

Symmetric Corner.

To edit a node:

1. Select it with the **Node Edit Tool**.

2. Drag its control handle(s) to fine-tune the curve.

To add a node, double-click on a line segment. To remove a selected node, press the **Delete** key.

 Use the 🗍 **Straighten Line** button to make a line segment straight.

Creating and editing text

PhotoPlus makes use of two text tools, i.e.

- The **T** **Text Tool**, for entering solid text on a new layer. Use for eye-catching or subtle captioning (opposite) and titling equally.

- The **T** **Text Selection Tool**, for creating a selection in the shape of text (for filling with unusual fills).

To create new solid text:

1.   **T ⋅ T** Click the **Text Tools** flyout on the **Tools** toolbar and choose the standard **Text Tool**.

2.   Click on your image with the text cursor to set where you want to insert text. Then set text attributes on the Text Context toolbar.
     - or -

     Drag across the page to size your text according to requirements.

3.   Type your text. The text appears on a new transparent Text Layer shown in the Layers tab. You can now use the Move Tool or other tools and commands to manipulate it, just like the contents of any layer.

To edit existing text:

1. With the text layer to be edited as the active layer, choose the standard **Text Tool** and move the mouse pointer over the text until it changes to the (I-beam) cursor.

2. Click on or drag to select areas of text—this lets you insert or overwrite selected text, respectively. Equally, you can set new text attributes to be adopted by the selected text area—all made from the Text Context toolbar.

To change text's solid colour:

1. Select all or part of any text.

2. Click the colour swatch on the Context toolbar to display the Colour Selector dialog. (See Choosing colours on p. 103.)

3. Select your new colour and click **OK**.

To swap to a gradient colour:

This applies a gradient fill to all of your text on the layer and not to selected text.

1. On the **Layers** tab, right-click the Text layer and choose **Edit Fill**.

2. Change the **Fill Type** from **Solid** to one of Linear, Radial, Conical, or Square.

3. Click on the **Fill** gradient swatch and select a preset gradient fill or create your own gradient from the dialog.

To convert any text layer to a standard layer:

*   Right-click on the layer name and choose **Rasterize** from the menu.

To create a text selection:

1.   **T** ▾ ⊤ Click the **Text Tools** flyout (**Tools** toolbar) and choose the **Text Selection Tool**.

2.   Click at the location on the image where you want to begin the selection.

   - or -

   Drag across the page to size your text selection. Release the mouse button to set the point size.

3.   (Optional) On the Text context toolbar, set the selection text attributes to be adopted by the new selection.

4.   Type your text directly onto the page.

5.   When you're done, click the ⊘ **OK** button on the Context toolbar. A selection marquee appears around the text's outline.

6.   You can now cut, copy, move, modify, and of course fill the selection.

Colour and Greyscale

8

Choosing colours

Foreground and background colours

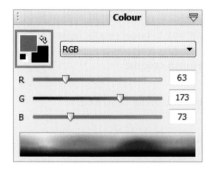

At any given time, PhotoPlus allows you to work with just two colours—a **foreground** colour and a **background** colour. These are always visible as two square swatches.

The foreground colour is set to green (RGB 63:173:73) and the background colour to black.

The **Colour tab** makes it possible to set the working colour model before colour selection: **RGB** (Red, Green, Blue); **CMYK** (Cyan, Magenta, Yellow, Black); **HSB** sliders (Hue, Saturation, Brightness); **HSL** sliders (Hue, Saturation, Lightness); **HSL** Colour Wheel; **HSL** Colour Box; **Greyscale**; or **Lab**.

To set the model:

- Choose an option from the RGB drop-down list.

Defining colours

Now, a few things to remember about how these colours are used:

- When you draw a selection, shape, or use the paintbrush tools, you apply the foreground colour.

- However, the black text in the design could be created after swapping foreground and background colours using the tab's ⟲ button. Loading the foreground and background colour with two frequently used colours is a great way to boost productivity.

To define foreground and background colour:

1. Select the ✎ **Colour Pickup Tool** on the Tools toolbar.

   As you move the cursor around your photo, a swatch appears displaying the colour under the cursor.

R:252 G:179 B:0 O:255

2. (Optional) On the Context toolbar, set the **Sample Size** (pickup region) as a single "Point Sample", "3 x 3 Average" or "5 x 5 Average" area. The last two options let you sample an "averaged" colour over a square pixel region.

3. Left-click with the tool anywhere on an image to "pick up" the colour at that point as the new foreground colour. Right-click to define a new background colour.

- or -

1. On the Colour tab, click and drag the mouse pointer (dropper cursor) around the **Colour Spectrum**. The tab's active colour swatch updates to the colour at the cursor position.

2. Left-click in the spectrum to set a new foreground colour, and right-click to set a new background colour.

If you want to add any colour to your photo you will have to reopen the file in PhotoPlus.

Colour modes

PhotoPlus operates in several colour modes to let you work in standard and higher levels of colour or tonal detail—these are 8 Bits/Channel RGB (or 8 Bits/Channel Greyscale), the more detailed 16 Bits/Channel RGB (or 16 Bits/Channel Greyscale), and Lab 16 Bits/Channel mode for professional yet natural edits.

As a rule of thumb, use RGB 8 Bits/Channel for general editing, then consider RGB 16 Bits/Channel or Lab mode for deep colour or professional edits.

If you already have 16-bit images, you'll probably want to benefit from that deep colour or tonal information throughout your project, from opening, through editing, to saving your high quality images.

PhotoPlus also lets you **manually** choose modes:

	Choose..	Then select
When creating a new image	**New Image** (Startup Assistant) or **File>New**	Colour Mode: RGB, Lab or Greyscale Bit Depth: 8 or 16 bits per channel
At any time	**Image>Colour Mode**	RGB 8 Bits/Channel RGB 16 Bits/Channel Lab 8 Bits/Channel Lab 16 Bits/Channel Greyscale 8 Bits/Channel Greyscale 16 Bits/Channel
Importing raw images	from the **Bit Depth** drop-down list (**Output Format**)	8 Bits/Channel 16 Bits/Channel
When outputting HDR Merge results	**File>HDR Merge**.	Output 16-bits per channel

If you don't need to work at the highest level of colour or detail (Lab or RGB 16 Bits/channel), you can use RGB 8-bit mode, which results in smaller file sizes and allows you to use PhotoPlus's full range of special filter effects.

To switch from Lab or RGB 16 Bits/Channel to RGB 8 Bits/Channel working:

- From the **Image** menu, select **Colour Mode**, and select an 8 Bits/Channel option from the submenu.

To check which mode is currently set, the Title bar shows the mode after the file name, zoom, and image size.

Printing and Exporting

9

Printing

For basic printing primarily to desktop printers, **Print Studio** offers an exciting, comprehensive, and versatile printing solution for your photos.

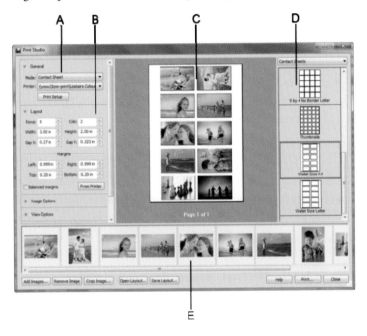

A - Print Mode, B - Print Mode Options, C - Page Layout, D - Templates, E - Open Images

The easy-to-use studio environment lets you select from a variety of print templates, each designed for either single or multi-image printing. Multi-image printing in PhotoPlus lets you make the most of expensive photo-quality printing paper by "grouping" several images onto a single output sheet using a **print layout** or **contact sheet** template (shown above).

- **Single Image templates**

  Use for basic desktop printing of an individual image, with supporting Layout options (custom or standard print sizes, positioning, tiling, and image-to-cell fitting).

- **Print Layout templates**

  Use for multi-image standard print sizes (in portrait/landscape orientation), passport sizes, and mixed print sizes.

- **Contact Sheet templates**

  Use for multi-image template-driven thumbnail prints—great for creating labels!

For any mode, you can also create your own custom template from an existing template.

Currently open documents will be used for printing, although you can add more directly within Print Studio.

To print (using templates):

1. Click the 🖶 **Print** button on the **Standard** toolbar. The Print Studio appears.

2. (Optional) To open additional images for printing, click **Add Images**. Select a photo for addition then click **Open**. The images are added as a thumbnail to the gallery.

3. From the right-hand templates list, select a template category, e.g. Single Images (Portrait).

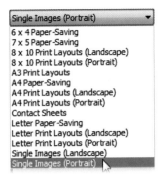
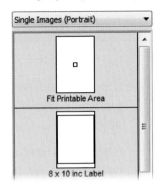

4. To insert a particular template into the central page layout region, simply click its gallery thumbnail.

5. Depending on print mode, decide on which image(s) are to be used for printing, i.e.

- For **Single Image** templates, you can select a different image from the lower image gallery.

- For **Print Layout** templates, right-click a gallery thumbnail and select **Fill Layout with Image**. All occupied or empty cells in your layout are filled with the selected image. Alternatively, to fill an individual cell, drag a replacement image from the lower image gallery onto the "target" cell..

- For **Contact Sheet** templates, use the **Distribution** option in **Image Options** to control image replacement.

6. (Optional) From the left-hand pane, click the ▶ button to expand **Image Options** for sizing and rotating images (see below) in cells:

- Enable **Fit image to cell** to make the image fit within the cell boundaries.

- Enable **Fill cell with image** to scale the image to fit all of the cell.

- Check **Rotate for best fit** to make portrait images fit cells of landscape orientation (and vice versa) to make maximum use of cell space.

7. (Optional) Check **Border** to add a border of a configurable width (use input box) and Colour (click the swatch to select colour from a dialog).

8. (Optional) To caption your images, check **Label.** Then, from the drop-down list, select either the Date, image Filename, or Sequence number to appear under each image. For a combination of label formats, click **Modify**, add tokens to assemble a sample name, then click **OK** and the drop-down list automatically changes to Custom.

9. Click **Print**, or click **Close** to save settings (without printing).

If you want to create your own layouts instead of templates you can switch print modes and customize settings for that mode.

To print using your own layouts:

1. Click the 🖶 **Print** button on the **Standard** toolbar. The Print Studio appears.

2. From the **Mode** drop-down list, select Single Image, Print Layout, or Contact Sheet.

3. In the Layout section, set a custom or standard print size.

4. (Optional) Follow image sizing and rotating instructions described above.

Exporting to another file format

In many situations, you'll want to save a file to one of the standard graphics formats. In PhotoPlus, this is known as **exporting**.

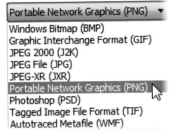

Exporting converts your image to a specified graphic file format (opposite) other than the native PhotoPlus (SPP) format. This flattens it, removing layer information.

Only SPP and Photoshop PSD formats preserves image information, such as multiple layers, masks, or image map data.

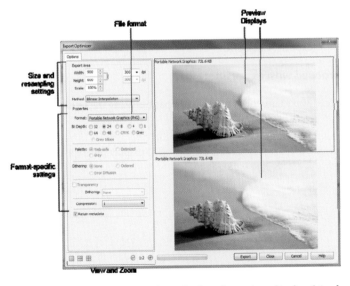

The Export Optimizer consists of a right-hand preview display (single, dual, or quad) and a left-hand settings region. Dual and quad previews let you test and compare between different export formats in each pane—simply select a preview pane and then test various quality settings, change format-specific options or resize before going ahead with your optimized file's export!

Exporting images

To export an image:

1. From the **File** menu, select **Export**.

2. In the Export Optimizer dialog, use the **Options** tab to specify the **Export Area**, resampling method, file **Format**, and format-specific options such as bit depth, dithering, palette, and compression.

3. Review your optimized image, and when you're happy with it, click **Export**.

4. From the Save As dialog, choose a folder and enter a file name. The export format and custom settings will be remembered for future exports. Click **OK**.

To proceed with exporting:

1. Make sure the active preview pane is using the settings you want to apply to the image.

2. Click the dialog's **Export** button to display the Export dialog.

Additional Information

10

Contacting Serif

Help with your Product

On the web	
Com**M**unityPlus	**community.serif.com** Get answers and ask questions in the Serif community! Type 'PhotoPlus X7' to filter PhotoPlus only articles.

Additional Serif information

On the web	
Serif website	**www.serif.com**
Main office	
Address	The Software Centre, PO Box 2000 Nottingham, NG11 7GW, UK
Phone	(0115) 914 2000
Phone (Registration)	(0800) 376 1989 +44 800 376 1989 800-794-6876 (US, Canada)
Phone (Sales)	(0800) 376 7070 +44 800 376 7070 800-489-6703 (US, Canada)
Customer Service	0845 345 6770 800-489-6720 (US, Canada)
Fax	(0115) 914 2020

Credits

This User Guide, and the software described in it, is furnished under an end user License Agreement, which is included with the product. The agreement specifies the permitted and prohibited uses.

Trademarks

Serif is a registered trademark of Serif (Europe) Ltd.

PhotoPlus is a registered trademark of Serif (Europe) Ltd.

All Serif product names are trademarks of Serif (Europe) Ltd.

Microsoft, Windows and the Windows logo are registered trademarks of Microsoft Corporation. All other trademarks acknowledged.

Windows Vista and the Windows Vista Start button are trademarks or registered trademarks of Microsoft Corporation in the United States and/or other countries.

Adobe Photoshop is a registered trademark of Adobe Systems Incorporated in the United States and/or other countries.

Copyrights

Digital Images © 2008 Hemera Technologies Inc. All Rights Reserved.

Portions Images ©1997-2002 Nova Development Corporation; ©1995 Expressions Computer Software; ©1996-98 CreatiCom, Inc.; ©1996-99 Cliptoart; ©1997 Multimedia Agency Corporation; ©1997-98 Seattle Support Group. Rights of all parties reserved.

The Radiance Software License, Version 1.0
Copyright © 1990 - 2002 The Regents of the University of California, through Lawrence Berkeley National Laboratory. All rights reserved.

This product includes Radiance software (http://radsite.lbl.gov/) developed by the Lawrence Berkeley National Laboratory (http://www.lbl.gov/).

Copyright © 2002-2011, Industrial Light & Magic, a division of Lucasfilm Entertainment Company Ltd. All rights reserved.

PhotoPlus Organizer was developed using LEADTOOLS, copyright ©1991-2007 LEAD Technologies, Inc. All Rights Reserved.

Serif PhotoPlus X7 © 2014 Serif (Europe) Ltd. All rights reserved.

Index